AUSTRALIA'S COAST

PHOTOGRAPHS FROM THE AUSTRALIAN GEOGRAPHIC IMAGE COLLECTION

CONTENTS

OPPOSITE: ***One Tree Coconut Beach, Lizard Island, Qld.*** MIKE MCCOY
From Lizard Island's granite beach boulders, the view to the south takes in neighbouring Palfrey Island and, at left, South Island.

Forest Lagoon, Bathurst Harbour, Tas. PETER MCNEILL

Deep in Tasmania's South-west wilderness, 15km from the open sea, a tinny and vessel sit
in Bathurst Harbour. The harbour formed about 18,000 years ago when seas rose.

INTRODUCTION

For three-quarters of Australians, home is within cooee of the coast. Our land is girt by sea and we are the world's largest island nation; no wonder the beach is part of our national pysche.

THE COAST is Australia's face to the world. And it's a countenance that's ever changing. With beaches like broad, sandy grins, cliffs that scowl, bristly mangrove shores and clear, blue-eyed bays, our outward features never fail to express.

Including its castaway islands, Australia's perimeter stretches for nearly 60,000km — enough to lap the equator one and a half times. Of this tally, 94 per cent of the coast rolls wild and free, barely altered by humankind.

From capes and estuaries to reefs, gulfs and coral cays, the continent is fringed in lavish detail. Yet, up close, the experience along this edge is less about its facets than natural forces in full flight; pumping tides and rip-roaring surf, winter gales and thunderous summer storms. Above all else these margins swirl with the restless cycle of life, the myriad creatures working the thresholds between land and open sea.

It's a zone Australians are inextricably wedded to. More than 80 per cent of our population lives less than 100km from the coast. Every state capital city has its own affinity with glinting water views or sea breezes. Deeper still are our time-honoured ties to waves and sand. Australia has a remarkable 10,700 beaches. They occupy almost half the total length of our coast. Some are wedged in tiny coves; some mark the watery limit of densely populated city suburbs and yet others are rollicking strips of surf and dazzling dunes such as the Coorong and the self-proclaiming Eighty Mile and Ninety Mile beaches.

With such abundance it's little wonder that the coast serves as the nation's sunlit front verandah. No other space can match its democratic, freewheeling spirit. Here we're always on the brink of something big: fish, waves to ride, humpbacks breaching, dolphins riding the bow, spinnaker runs, shells to treasure. It's the place where our dreams run barefoot and luck feels like a promise made fresh every day.

NORTH

Australia's tropics stretch from the Kimberley in the west to Far North Queensland in the east, taking in the the Top End along the way.

THEY'RE OUR closest bridge to the outside world, a wartime frontline and the ancient landing points for the first Australians. Yet these significant northern reaches form our most enigmatic border. Indeed, they flourish as one of the wildest frontiers left on Earth. It's also where we come closest to sharing a border — Papua New Guinea's just in view.

The natural defences are formidable: a maze of reefs and islands, rugged sandstone battlements and a snaking shoreline fretted by rivers and floodplains. This is the kingdom of a master predator — the saltwater crocodile, the largest living reptile. It's also a realm of extremes; blistering tropical heat, 11m tides, wet season deluges and brutal cyclonic storms.

As well as these turmoils, this is also a place of quiet, intricate beauty, be it the vivacious life of coral reefs, sheltered bays where dugongs graze or pale sand beaches where baby turtles hatch. To linger on these shores through the blush of sundown is to witness colour made indelible: milky turquoise shallows, rainforest greens and cliffs in ochre hues.

For more than 50,000 years the north has endured as a heartland for the world's oldest continuous culture. To the 'saltwater people' the seaward margin is not a boundary but a vital force in their art, hunting, music and Dreaming. For them, the coast and its rhythms are everything.

OPPOSITE: **Eastern clown anemonefish, Qld.** NICK RAINS
Growing up to 8cm long, these iconic reef fish are found in the northern Great Barrier Reef and New Guinea where they shelter in the waving fronds of a variety of host anemones.

Pelican Island, Gulf of Carpentaria, NT. MURRAY SPENCE
More than 4000 pelicans breed on this spit of white sand at the mouth of the Smithburne
River, in the south-east of the Gulf of Carpentaria.

Groote Eylandt, NT. EDWARD STOKES
Silhouetted on a silvery sea, a local Aboriginal fisherman steps gingerly through shallows in
the Gulf of Carpentaria, spear poised, ready to catch a feed.

Coconut Beach, Cape Tribulation, Qld.

ANDREW GREGORY

Early morning gilds the lines of gentle breakers at Coconut Beach, 80km north of Cairns.

Dwarf minke whale, Coral Sea, Qld. DARREN JEW
The torpedo-like body of a minke whale pierces the aquamarine waters of the northern
Great Barrier Reef. Growing to 8m, this species mates and gives birth in these warm waters.

Masked booby, Coral Sea, Qld. JASON EDWARDS
With a solid yellow bill, a wingspan up to 1.7m and blue webbed feet, the masked booby
is a distinctive character on islands in Australia's north.

Cape Leveque, Kimberley, WA. DICK SMITH
A 13m lighthouse stands atop the fiery red cliffs at Cape Leveque on the
Dampier Peninsula, 150km north-east of Broome.

Bigeye with blue cleaner fish, Great Barrier Reef, Qld. MIKE MCCOY
A nocturnal fish, the bigeye tends to shelter in caves and ledges during the day. Despite its
relatively large mouth, it eats only tiny zooplankton.

*Cowrie Beach,
Daintree NP, Qld.*

ANDREW GREGORY

A red mangrove
weaves a tangled
web of salt-filtering
roots on Cowrie
Beach, northern
Queensland.

Hard coral, Great Barrier Reef, Qld. MIKE MCCOY
Like small lilac antlers, the branches of a hard coral, *Seriatophora hystrix*, sometimes called
birdsnest coral, reach out in every direction. The reef contains some 360 hard coral species.

Pincushion starfish, Great Barrier Reef, Qld. MIKE MCCOY
Resembling an Aboriginal dot painting, this close-up of a pincushion starfish on the
Great Barrier Reef shows the mouth area, at centre.

SOUTH

Unrelenting wind and waves characterise our southern reaches, where vast stretches of remote, wild coastline reveal only the occasional human footprint.

IT TOOK 50 million years for Antarctica and Australia to tear apart. This final chapter in Gondwana's break-up didn't merely launch the island continent. It also opened up the Southern Ocean, unleashing its circumpolar current — the biggest weather engine on the planet.

Fast forward 30 million years and the impact of these upheavals are plain to see. From the Nullarbor's storm-ravaged cliffs, to wind-pruned vegetation on Tasmania's west coast, the whirling westerlies of the Southern Ocean have etched their mark.

Throughout the 19th century these same winds bore European vessels along our southern shores. With every decade this coast's fearsome reputation for gales and shipwrecks gathered strength — especially around Bass Strait. Some 77 lighthouses now mark the great arc of hazards between Cape Leeuwin and Gabo Island: beacons to the haunting power of these waters.

For all its unruliness, the Southern Ocean remains the great provider. It's a lively habitat for everything from whales, seals and penguins, to prized bounty such as lobster, prawns, abalone and tuna. Similarly, the very winds and waves that yachties and fishermen grapple with, have carved out tranquil havens tucked along these granite and limestone shores — sheltered bays where refuge tastes all the sweeter for knowing the wildness beyond.

OPPOSITE: **Sandy Cape, Tarkine Coast, Tas.** JOE SHEMESH
Huge waves generated by powerful Southern Ocean winds have sculpted this section of coastline, in north-western Tasmania, into rugged bays and spectacular sand dunes.

Surprise Bay, South Coast Track, Tas. DON FUCHS
Tilted rock shelves and tannin-stained creeks meet the ocean at Surprise Bay, one of the
remote camping sites on the legendary South Coast Track in south-west Tasmania.

Cape Conran, East Gippsland, Vic. DON FUCHS
On Victoria's east coast, bright lichen seems to have been sprayed across the jagged
siltstone and sandstone like orange paint. Each lichen is a special blend of fungus and algae.

Lakes Entrance, Vic. DON FUCHS
Reflections of fishing trawlers tied up in the safety of Lakes Entrance, eastern Victoria,
shine and shimmer under a speckled sky.

The cray fleet, Kettering, Tas. PAUL NEVIN
Just after dawn, crayfishermen on the Derwent River at Kettering, Tasmania,
prepare the pots and lines before heading out to sea.

Shipwreck Creek, Croajingolong NP, Vic.

DON FUCHS

Forming a horseshoe in the sand, the brandy-coloured Shipwreck Creek winds down to the Pacific Ocean in Croajingolong National Park.

Sea lion colony, Baird Bay, SA. DARREN JEW
Like languorous sculptures, sea lions lounge around at various haul-out spots on the SA
coastline and offshore islands, including Kangaroo Island and Baird Bay.

Picnic Point, Bay of Fires, Tas. ESTHER BEATON
Sculpted granite boulders offset a stunning aquamarine sea at Picnic Point in
Mount William National Park, north-eastern Tasmania.

Lichens, Flinders Island, Tas. DON FUCHS
Looking like an abstract painting, a variety of brightly coloured lichens compete on a granite
boulder on Flinders Island, the largest island in Bass Strait.

Trousers Point, Flinders Island, Tas. DON FUCHS
The ragged outline of the Strzelecki Peaks looms over the quiet waters and rugged
boulders of Trousers Point, on Flinders' Island's south-west.

Royal penguin colony, Macquarie Island. JASMINE POOLE
In cold conditions 1300km south-east of Tasmania, hundreds of royal penguins make an
artistic pattern in the mist with their black and white coats, and distinctive orange plumes.

Sea kelp, Tas. ROB WALLS
Streamers of bull kelp dry on racks near Currie, on King Island, Bass Strait. It is turned into
alginate and used to produce shampoo, ice-cream, beer, cosmetics and medicinal creams.

EAST

It's where modern Australia began and, despite its proximity to so much humanity, it's still easy to find peace and solitude along our eastern seaboard.

EVERY SWISH and tuck on this hem of the continent reveals a new look. Here a scallop of sand, there a forest fringe or the pleat of a river inlet. From high-rise towers to castaway isles this is truly a coast of many colours.

Australia's starboard side is also a busy place. With its seaside towns and resorts — plus a welter of suburbs camped by the water's edge — this seaboard can appear idealised, even overworked. However, below the high-water mark, old beach traditions hold fast.

In the end, glitz is no match for booming breakers or the grounding truth of sinking toes into sand. For many a coast dweller, a tingling morning dip is a daily devotion — life as an endless surf carnival.

Time has shaped this ancient, drowned landscape with a glorious succession of bluffs, bays and deep harbours. The other great gift to beachgoers is out of sight: the whirling East Australian Current bringing warm water south from the Coral Sea.

It's a reminder this is the mercurial coast of reinvention, where flooding rivers charge out to sea, shifting sands create wondrous forms, and corals spawn to refresh the miracle that is the Great Barrier Reef.

OPPOSITE: **Pittwater, NSW.** ESTHER BEATON

Cormorants dry their wings on bollards on the Hawkesbury River just north of Sydney. For many years the river supplied water to Sydney's food basket.

Crayfish Beach, Hook Island, Qld. ANDREW GREGORY
The Whitsunday Islands have glorious hidden camping sites, with fringing coral reefs, for
well-prepared boaters and kayakers. This is Crayfish Beach on the east side of Hook Island.

Wattamolla, Royal NP, NSW. ESTHER BEATON
A popular picnic spot south of Sydney, Wattamolla sits in Australia's oldest national park.
Signs prohibit jumping off the falls, but many still do.

Fishing shack, Stockton Beach, Newcastle, NSW. PETER MCNEILL
Massive, wind-blown dunes tower over a corrugated iron shack on Stockton Beach, north of
Newcastle. Owners of the 11 shacks here have to constantly keep the moving sand at bay.

Longboarding, Newcastle, NSW. PETER AITCHISON
Professional longboarder Belinda Baggs and her father Phil
check out the swell around Newcastle.

Hinchinbrook Island, Qld.

BILL BACHMAN

Mangroves form a maze in the mudflats in front of Hinchinbrook Island, which is about 5km off the coast between Townsville and Cairns.

Nippers, Coogee Beach, NSW. FRANCES MOCNIK
During a weekend Surf Life Saving Australia race, an Under-11 competitor sprints for the
breakers, which are gentle today. He'll paddle 170m out to two markers, and then return.

Nippers, Coogee Beach, NSW. FRANCES MOCNIK
The Under-9 ranks of the Coogee Surf Life Saving Australia club take to the surf for a
swimming race on an overcast Sydney morning.

Sandblow, Fraser Island. ANDREW GREGORY
The world's largest sand island, Fraser has a series of large sandblows on its east coast
that overtake the vegetation and form giant sand dunes.

Lord Howe Island, NSW. DICK AND PIP SMITH
A stunning World Heritage Area off the NSW coast, Lord Howe Island has coral bays,
lush rainforests, rare birdlife and mountains that rise up to 875m from the sea.

***South Molle,
Whitsunday
Islands, Qld.***

ANDREW GREGORY

South Molle is
one of the closest
Whitsunday Islands
to the mainland. It
holds both a resort
and some isolated
bush camping spots.

WEST

From pearls to stromatolites and dolphins to whale sharks — head into the west to find delights aplenty — where the red of the outback meets the blue sea.

WILD, IMPOSING and vivid — this is coast on an epic scale. In contrast to the east's hectic changes, here the shores unfold in mighty sweeps of cliff, bay and dune. It's as if the continent has finally found a profile to match the immensity of the interior.

Indeed, for long stretches this coast goes toe-to-toe with the outback. Bleached spinifex plains and red deserts tumble into white-sand beaches. Further north, the Pilbara's chocolate-red ironstone ridges butt against bright, sapphire seas.

Exposed to blazing light and buffeting sea breezes, these shores were a daunting prospect to the Dutch sailors who first spied them. Four centuries on and the west retains a sparse, no-nonsense look. This is a working coast scattered with mining ports, roadhouses and sun-struck fishing towns. Home might be a galvo shack, or a flapping caravan awning. What matters is out on the water: surf breaking, fish schooling, catching the tide in a tinny.

We've learned to absorb the west's fierce beauty. But the essence here is elemental. The delicious freedom of untrodden sand, haunting, salt-bitten spaces for watching birds and our daily closing ceremony: the Indian Ocean swallowing the sun.

OPPOSITE: **Green turtle, Ningaloo Reef, WA.** ANDREW GREGORY
In Australia's second-biggest coral reef system, a green turtle glides over a forest of branching coral inhabited by humbugs and other small tropical fishes.

Windmills, Cape Naturaliste, WA. ANDREW GREGORY
Windmills, just south of Cape Naturaliste in south-west WA, is washed with huge swells.
The waves here attract experienced surfers from around the world.

Rottnest tea-trees, Bunker Bay, WA. ANDREW GREGORY
Rottnest tea-trees, contorted and stripped by strong winds, line Bunker Bay, on the
north-east side of Cape Naturaliste.

Dolphin encounter, Monkey Mia, WA. PAUL RAFFAELE
Ranger Marika Maxwell interacts with one of the wild bottlenose dolphins that
regularly swim in to meet the crowds at Monkey Mia, Shark Bay.

Crayfisherman, Dongara, WA. THOMAS WIELECKI
Veteran deckie Doug Bowen shows off some of the 140kg of lobster retrieved on the lobster
boat *Wave Cruiser*, which operates out of Dongara, 350km north of Perth.

***Turquoise Bay,
Ningaloo region,
WA***

ANDREW GREGORY
In the calm waters
of Turquoise Bay,
holidaymakers
swim and snorkel
right off the beach.

Vlamingh Head Lighthouse, Cape Range NP, WA.

ANDREW GREGORY
Built from local stone, the Vlamingh Head Lighthouse has been a sentinel on the coast north of Exmouth since 1912.

Heirisson Prong, Shark Bay, WA. JIRI LOCHMAN
Speckled with scrub and sand, Heirisson Prong is a thin sliver of land piercing
the crystal-clear waters of Shark Bay, WA.

Salt harvesting, Useless Loop, Shark Bay, WA. JIRI LOCHMAN
About 1.6 million tonnes of pure sea salt are produced here annually. The wholly natural
process uses only the wind and the heat of the sun to extract salt from pristine sea water.

Pearling lugger, Broome, WA. RORY MCGUINNESS
On waters like gold silk fabric, a timber pearling lugger heads for port.
Broome's pearling history dates back to the 1880s.

Trannies Beach, Cocos (Keeling) Islands. DON FUCHS
Australia's most westerly outpost, the 27 Cocos (Keeling) Islands are closer to Sri Lanka
than to mainland Australia. Trannies Beach is on West Island, one of two inhabited islands.

Australian GEOGRAPHIC

AUSTRALIA'S COAST

PHOTOGRAPHS FROM THE AUSTRALIAN GEOGRAPHIC IMAGE COLLECTION

All the photographs featured in this book can be ordered as high quality photographic prints.
For details and prices, please visit www.australiangeographicprints.com.au

MANAGING EDITOR, AUSTRALIAN GEOGRAPHIC COMMERCIAL: Chrissie Goldrick
BOOK DESIGN: Mike Rossi CREATIVE DIRECTOR: Andrew Burns
WRITERS: Quentin Chester, Ken Eastwood, Chrissie Goldrick
SUB-EDITOR: Josephine Sargent PROOFREADER: Nina Paine
PRODUCTION MANAGER: Victoria Jefferys PREPRESS: Klaus Müller
AUSTRALIAN GEOGRAPHIC GENERAL MANAGER: Jo Runciman
AUSTRALIAN GEOGRAPHIC EDITOR: Ian Connellan

ACP MANAGING DIRECTOR: Matthew Stanton PUBLISHING DIRECTOR: Gerry Reynolds
PUBLISHER: Andrew Stedwell CEO, NINE ENTERTAINMENT CO.: David Gyngell

Printed in China by Everbest Printing Co.Ltd.

© ACP Magazines Ltd 2012

Published by ACP Magazines Ltd, 54–58 Park Street, Sydney, NSW 2000
Australian Geographic customer service 1300 555 176 (Australia only)

www.australiangeographic.com.au

AUTHOR: Chester, Quentin.
TITLE: Australia's coast: images from the Australian Geographic image collection / Quentin Chester, Ken Eastwood, Chrissie Goldrick.
ISBN: 9781742453187 (hbk.)
SUBJECTS: Australian Geographic Pty. Ltd.--Coasts--Australia--Pictorial works.

OTHER AUTHORS/CONTRIBUTORS: Eastwood, Ken. Goldrick, Chrissie. Australian Geographic Pty Ltd.

DEWEY NUMBER: 919.4

Other titles in the series Photographs from the Australian Geographic Image Collection:
Australia in Colour, Landscapes of Australia, Outback Australia

FRONT COVER:
Cowrie Beach, Daintree NP, Qld
ANDREW GREGORY

A stunning red mangrove's solitary form stands on sand-flats at Cowrie Beach.

TITLE PAGE:
Seal Creek, Croajingolong NP, Vic.
DON FUCHS

Forest tannins leach into the water at Croajingolong, creating tea-coloured creeks.

BACK COVER:
Sea lions, SA
DARREN JEW

Found only in SA and WA waters, Australian sea lions are social animals, usually gathering in groups of 10–15.